Adam and Eve

Story by Penny Frank

Illustrated by Tony Morris

THE LION
STORY BIBLE

2

TRING · BELLEVILLE · SYDNEY

The very first story
in the Bible tells us that when God
made the earth it was good. He made
a man and a woman — Adam and
Eve — who lived in a beautiful
garden.
This story tells us what happened
when Adam and Eve disobeyed God.
You can find the story in your own
Bible, in Genesis chapter 3.

Copyright © 1985 Lion Publishing

Published by
Lion Publishing plc
Icknield Way, Tring, Herts, England
ISBN 0 85648 727 9
Lion Publishing Corporation
10885 Textile Road, Belleville,
Michigan 48111, USA
ISBN 0 85648 727 9
Albatross Books
PO Box 320, Sutherland, NSW 2232, Australia
ISBN 0 86760 511 1

First edition 1985

Printed and bound in Hong Kong
by Mandarin Offset International (HK) Ltd

**British Library Cataloguing in
Publication Data**

Frank, Penny
    Adam and Eve. – (The Lion Story
Bible; 2)
    1. Adam *(Biblical character)* –
Juvenile literature
    2. Eve *(Biblical character)* – Juvenile
literature
    2. Bible stories, English – O.T.
Genesis
    I. Title   II. Series
222'.110922   BS580

ISBN 0-85648-727-9

**Library of Congress Cataloging in
Publication Data**

Frank, Penny.
    Adam and Eve.
    (The Lion Story Bible; 2)
    1. Adam (Biblical figure)—Juvenile
literature. 2. Eve (Biblical figure)—
Juvenile literature. [1. Adam (Biblical
figure) 2. Eve (Biblical figure) 3. Bible
stories—O.T.] I. Morris, Tony, ill.
II. Title. III. Series: Frank, Penny.
Lion Story Bible; 2.
BS580.A4F73 1985   222'.1109505
84-26125
ISBN 0-85648-727-9

In the very first days, when the earth
was young, God walked in his beautiful
garden.

He loved to see all the animals he had
made. Most of all he loved to come and
visit the man and woman he had made.
They were his friends. Their names were
Adam and Eve.

God usually came to see them in the evening before it was dark, when the air was cool.

They told him what they had been doing in the day.

Adam and Eve enjoyed the garden God
had made. They looked after the plants.
They picked the fruit and berries
when they were ripe.

God had said that the earth was for them to enjoy. They had chosen the names for the animals. They played with them. They splashed in the river. They watched the clouds.

'You may eat the fruit of all the trees in the garden,' God said, 'except that one tree in the middle.'

It was easy to obey, because there were plenty of other good things to eat.

All the animals loved Adam and Eve.
They were not afraid of each other.
    But there was one who was different.
He was a cunning snake. He was not
happy when he saw that the man and
woman were friends with God.

One day, when Eve was in the garden, the cunning snake said, 'Why don't you taste the fruit from the tree in the middle of the garden? Didn't God say you could have anything you wanted to eat?'

'We can eat anything from any of these
beautiful trees and plants,' said Eve,
'but we must never eat the fruit of
that tree, or we will die.'

'How silly you are to believe that!' hissed the cunning snake. 'You won't die! If you eat that fruit you will know as much as God. Try it, and see that I am right.'

Eve slowly turned and went to the tree.
She put her arms around it and looked
up into the leaves.

The fruit was red and shiny. In the
light of the sun it was beautiful.
It hung down quite low. She could
just reach it.

Eve took the fruit and bit it. 'It is
really delicious,' she said.

The cunning snake crept under a bush
and watched her.

Soon Adam came to look for her. He
found her under the tree, eating the fruit.
'This is better than all the other
fruit,' she said. 'You taste it.'
She held the fruit out and the man
bit it.

Then the cunning snake smiled. But Adam and Eve felt suddenly afraid.

They made clothes out of leaves to cover themselves.

'Oh dear,' they said. 'When God comes to visit us he will know we have disobeyed him. We must hide quickly.'

They had never hidden from God before, because they were his friends.

When God came in the evening, he called out, 'Where are you? Why are you afraid? Have you eaten the fruit of the tree in the middle of the garden?'

Adam and Eve came slowly out from
their hiding-place.

'Why did you eat that fruit?' said
God.

Adam pointed at Eve.

'She made me,' he said.

God said to Eve, 'Why did you eat the fruit?'

Eve pointed at the cunning snake. 'He made me,' she said.

God said to Adam and Eve. 'You have spoiled all my plans for you, because you have disobeyed me. Now you must go from my garden for ever. From now on you will have to work hard. You will feel pain. I will never be able to meet you here again. And when you grow old, you will die.'

So Adam and Eve were sent away from the garden. God was sad that he could not trust them.

The man and the woman were sad that they had disobeyed God.

It was hard work to grow their own food.
They were sad that the animals did not
trust them any more.

But most of all they missed having
God as their friend.

The Lion Story Bible is made up of 52 individual stories for young readers, building up an understanding of the Bible as one story — God's story — a story for all time and all people.

The Old Testament section (numbers 1–30) tells the story of a great nation — God's chosen people, the Israelites — and God's love and care for them through good times and bad. The stories are about people who knew and trusted God. From this nation came one special person, Jesus Christ, sent by God to save all people everywhere.

The story of *Adam and Eve* comes from the very beginning of the Bible, the Old Testament book of Genesis, chapters 2 and 3. It tells how God made man and woman to be in charge of his world and to enjoy a special relationship with himself. But Satan, the enemy of God, was already present in the beautiful new world that God had made. He tempted Adam and Eve to disobey God. So sin and death came in to spoil what had been so good, and mankind was separated from God.

But God still loved the people he had made. He had a plan to deal with sin and mend the broken relationship. His plan lay far in the future, with the coming of Jesus. But the next story in this series, number 3: *Noah and the great flood*, tells of a new beginning.